Open Minds, Open Hearts

A Journey With The Ages

By
Glenna C. Orr

With Maureen Allen

Illustrated by Nicole Mullins

Published by:

VSP Books Inc.
7402-G Lockport Place
Lorton, VA 22079

Order additional copies of *Open Minds, Open Hearts*
from your local bookstore,
or order copies from
Glenna Orr's website, www.TheKindKids.org,
or the publisher's website, www.VSPBooks.com,
or by calling VSP Books at **1-800-441-1949**.

Copyright © 2006 by Glenna C. Orr

All rights reserved. No part of this book may be reproduced in any form or by any electronic, video, digital or mechanical means, including information storage and retrieval systems, without permission in writing from the publisher, except by a reviewer, who may quote brief passages in a review.

ISBN 1-893622-18-5

Library of Congress Catalog Card Number: 2006923460

10 9 8 7 6 5 4 3 2 1

Printed in the United States of America

Dedication

Open Minds, Open Hearts: A Journey With The Ages is dedicated to my family, which has traveled at my side throughout the journeys.

~ **Glenna C. Orr**

Acknowledgements

Special thanks go to the following for helping make the publishing of this book a reality: Reading Is Fundamental of Northern Virginia; Strategic Insight, Ltd; American Equipment Company; The Washington Realty Group; Mrs. Virginia Crews; Mr. and Mrs. Peter & Joan Knetemann, and Mrs. Jo Ann Abrams.

Foreword

A Mother's Pride

It comes as no surprise that this author has written a book about a project, no—a cause, that for years has been so close to her heart. She set out at a very young age with aspirations of becoming a teacher who would make a difference.

She reached the station of teacher and set out, through her own creativity and determination, to instill a sense of awareness in her students about the plight of the less fortunate, elderly and the needy. To do this, she began to develop a plan to show students how they could bring compassion and comfort to those in need and a feeling of satisfaction to themselves.

The plan started so simply: Take the students on field trips to nursing homes, retirement centers, hospitals and anywhere else there was a need and expose them to the rewards of becoming a volunteer.

Glenna Orr

What she didn't plan on was how this project would grow and explode into a second full-time job.

Glenna spent untold hours contributing personal effort to make and keep the program alive and growing. She began to reach out to various organizations and individuals, soliciting them for support to open up more opportunities and ideas. The response was gratifying, to say the least. And the students were enthusiastic and responsive to this new concept of learning to become more aware of the contributions they could make to others.

And so one individual set out to add a whole other dimension to the lives of young people and I'm proud to say she reached that goal!

As Glenna's mother, I am very grateful that she has been able to chronicle this amazing journey. Hopefully all her efforts and sacrifices will inspire others to work with young people in this same direction.

~Virginia Crews

Table of Contents

Introduction		9
Chapter One	Once Upon a Morning Walk	11
Chapter Two	Coming Home	21
Chapter Three	On the Road Again	29
Chapter Four	Florida State University (FSU)	26
Chapter Five	Washington Mill and The Fairfax at Belvoir Woods	42
Chapter Six	Making a Promise	55
Chapter Seven	Carl Sandburg Middle School	64
Chapter Eight	Northern Virginia Community College	68
Chapter Nine	Hollin Hills	75
Closing Thoughts	Merely a Pause and Not an End	87
Epilogue	A Daughter's Praise	90
Appendix	Starting an Intergenerational Program	93

Introduction

Seniors and children, children and seniors—together. What a nice picture this makes, seeing both of these groups spending time together, sharing smiles. Imagine them together having fun, laughing, telling stories, singing songs, working on simple crafts, reading to each other. Think about the significance of this fun time shared between two groups of wonderful people—knowing that each has so much to learn from the other.

What began more than 20 years ago as a simple teaching career has become my lifelong journey. Ask any teacher, depending on the day, and I'm willing to bet that more often than not, he or she would tell you that the most rewarding aspect of teaching is making meaningful connections with students. I certainly agree, but I feel doubly enriched, because my work as a teacher has allowed me the fortunate opportunity to help establish similar connections between students and senior mentors.

This book is a collection of memories about events in time when intergenerational programs were created to bring together two distinct groups of people at very different stages of life: those who were just beginning their journeys and those who had a lifetime of experiences to share. Part of my goal in writing this book is to capture their voices and "hear" them describe their experiences in their own words.

Chapter One

Once Upon a Morning Walk

The language of friendship knows no borders

It was a beautiful fall day in Frankfurt, Germany. I remember vividly that the implied warmth of the crystal clear sky was countered by a crisp autumn nip in the air. The leaves on the trees were beginning to give way from the lush green of summer to a rusty reddish—brown.

Twenty-five first-graders, the majority of them children of United States military families living and working in Germany, were being led by me, their teacher turned eager tour guide, on a weekly walk around the local neighborhood. The walks were part of our regular routine and had been going on for several weeks, starting soon after the school year began in September 1986.

Our route was a simple three-block area around our school, but, for the enthusiastic first-graders, each trip meant another exciting outdoor adventure. During our walks, we frequently mingled with German citizens who were also out making their rounds through the neighborhood. Though our school was affiliated with the local Army base, it was located directly in a native German neighborhood, and the residents soon came to know the children, as well as base personnel, as regular fixtures on the scene.

In addition to enjoying the many interesting sights, sounds and smells of our adopted hometown, we'd also enjoy watching the German people sitting on balconies and porches, just enjoying the beauty of the day. It rains a lot around Frankfurt, so when the weather is nice, residents jump at the opportunity to take advantage of some time outdoors.

Glenna Orr

One of the landmarks on our route was a German retirement home, also called an "altersheim." It was easily identified as such because many of the residents—all senior citizens—frequently gathered on the residence's balcony to hold court over the goings—on in their neighborhood. After a few weeks of following our usual route past the retirement home, a few of the seniors began to wave at the children. The next time we passed, a few more joined in. Soon, nearly all of the seniors sitting on the balcony waved each day as we passed and, of course, the young children responded, with big smiles and hellos with eagerly—waving hands and arms in an international display of friendship.

To some, a wave may not mean much, but this simple gesture was the start of a remarkable relationship between my American students and the German seniors. After a few days of thinking about the two groups' sweet, wordless exchanges, I began to wonder what would happen if they actually met face to face. I had only been in the country a short time, but I was feeling adjusted to life abroad and I was ready to take on a new project. In fact, I felt drawn to it and began to sense that introducing my students to their senior neighbors might result in more than just a one-day get together.

I scheduled a meeting with my principal, Dr. Mabel Annerou, and prepared myself to make the case for this project. Much to my surprise, she didn't need a lot of convincing. Not only did she give me permission to contact the nursing home about organizing a visit, but she also used her base contacts to arrange transportation to and from the residence for the students.

With the principal's confidence behind me, I called the retirement home and spoke to the staff about the idea that I shared with Dr. Annerou. God must have been smiling on me that day because the staff couldn't have been more receptive. I was prepared for—and was fully expecting—some initial resistance to my suggestion. I wasn't fully competent in the existing cultural customs in Germany regarding treatment of the elderly and equally unsure how welcoming they would be to 25 boisterous American first-graders traipsing into their quiet space. However, the retirement home's doors were opened to us almost immediately.

Perhaps it was because the ties between the military base and its home community were good or perhaps it was out of mutual curiosity, but the first visit was a hit right from the start. As that gathering was mostly for introductions, we didn't have much on the agenda: just some smiles, hellos, handshakes and a simple craft project. All of the parents also were invited to join us so they could become familiar with our new project and feel comfortable letting their sons and daughters participate in the program. After that first meeting, the students were so excited about spending more time with their new friends that we planned—and made—a visit every month for the rest of the school year.

The way the retirement home was configured, patients were placed on floors depending on the severity of their care needs. Seniors who were the equivalent of assisted living residents lived on the lower floors, the severity of the cases advanced up the building, with the most frail, bed-ridden patients residing on the top floors. When the program began, only the seniors from the lower floors participated. Since this was a new experience for nearly all of my students, I didn't want to shock or upset them by putting them in situations that might seem frightening or unsettling. However, as the program progressed, I was amazed to see their confidence blossom to the point at which they frequently asked to see the rest of the nursing facility. Some even wanted to meet the sicker residents and made it a habit to check on them during their monthly visits to the home. This was just one of many wonderful examples of a barrier being overcome by the unquestioning acceptance of young people and their seemingly endless capacity to love.

In undertaking this project, I anticipated working hard to establish trust and cooperation among the school administrators, the nursing home staff and my students' parents. However, what I expected to be the most obvious barrier to our potential success was not even a factor. Most of the German seniors did not speak English, but there were a few students, as well as their parents, who spoke German. But guess what? It didn't matter. Language is not much of a barrier when there are smiles, music and fun to serve as the tools of communication. The friendships that seemed to sprout instantly on our first visit grew even stronger with each subsequent meeting. We enjoyed singing, telling stories that made everyone laugh and working together on small crafts and handy works. These were the little moments that helped form the glue that made this a true partnership between the ages. Parents of some of these first graders became regular helpers on our trips to the retirement home – and for many it became a family and community endeavor. A sense of family is particularly important when you live away from your own extended family, and the German seniors quickly filled the roles of surrogate grandparents to their young friends.

Christmas seems to be a universal favorite time of the year among children, even those living away from home. So, as the holidays approached, the students wanted to make extra visits and spend more time with their special friends during this special time of year. Warming cups of hot chocolate and traditional German cookies and candies shared among the seniors, students, and parents made the extra visits even more delightful. As yet another sign of their growing friendship, the first graders put their fingers to work and eagerly created holiday cards for each resident. A few weeks earlier, we had visited some German nurseries to gather old flowers and to make sweet-smelling baskets for each senior. Our new-found friends at the retirement home were so, so happy to receive their gifts-and the children were so proud to have delivered some holiday joy with their homemade Christmas goodies.

As we gathered to sing carols, in both German and English, our hearts were full of joy, and the true spirit of the season became even more real by watching it sparkle in the eyes of young and old alike.

Anyone who's ever had the experience of living abroad understands the need to make that place feel like home and to create the kinds of things that will make one's life full. For three years, this simple "intergenerational program" enchanted the lives of students, parents and residents of a retirement home in Frankfurt, Germany. These students began to learn at a very early age how wonderfully easy it is to give a little of themselves to others—others needier than they. In the process, both groups learned how easy it was to bridge the gap between cultures, make new friends and share different experiences.

Though he was not in my class, my son Ryan was one of the American students who took part in my intergenerational pilot program. If he gained nothing else from our experience abroad, I'm glad he had the opportunity to participate in this wonderful relationship-building experience. He can describe it best in his own words:

I remember the first time I went with my mom and her class to the retirement home in Frankfurt, Germany. I was younger, in fourth grade. I remember only a few distinct things about the day. It was sunny, the kids were discussing specific things with regard to the residents they had spent time with the previous week. I most remember the energy brought by the children into the home.

There was one woman who was a bit far along in her years, but whatever strength she had she found that day for 20 minutes with one of my mom's students. [The woman] was playful, smiling with every laugh a kid let go of, and talking of days when she was quick and excited about a future unknown. At least I guess that's what she was talking about. I don't speak German. You see, we were from the American schools on base in Frankfurt. This retirement home was in the middle of the city and none of the children spoke the language of the residents. But all a child had to do was show up and these very thankful residents had a day in their week that they cherished. It was a day for them to see the endless cycle they had been a part of and contributed to for close to a century. They may have even wondered how the child that was enlightening them all over again would factor in with the world they would shortly be leaving behind them. The connection was made because my mother decided the kids deserved more from their teacher than reading and arithmetic. They needed to be taught humility and respect for the world around them.

This was just the beginning of my trek. My program was simple and small in scale because I was just beginning to explore what could be done by uniting students and seniors. Looking back on it now—and considering how far this field has come—makes me so thankful that I followed my instincts nearly 20 years ago and didn't keep my "what if" to myself.

Chapter Two

Coming Home

Burke Lake Gardens

Living overseas can be difficult at times, but it can also be a wonderfully enriching, bonding experience for a family. My family was fortunate to have had the opportunity to savor all of the culture, flavor and personalities we discovered in Germany.

Open Minds, Open Hearts

But when our time at that overseas post expired, we were ready to come home. Among the many special memories and souvenirs that returned with us was the experience of starting the intergenerational program at the German retirement home. That was one particular aspect of our Germany experience that was hard to leave behind. However, I felt quite certain that it would not be my last time involved in such work.

Being a teacher, I fortunately often find work with little difficulty when I move to a new area. So when my family re-established itself in Northern Virginia on our return to the United States, I immediately looked for a job in the Fairfax County School System. Good fortune was on my side, and I secured a position teaching third grade at White Oaks Elementary School in Burke, Virginia. From 1989 to 1993, White Oaks would serve as my new educational home.

The beginning of my first school year at White Oaks was filled with several orientation activities: getting to know my new colleagues, my students and their parents and familiarizing myself with the culture of the school. While of my time was filled with teaching—and learning—I couldn't help but notice that something was missing. It was not long before I realized that I missed the time spent in Germany working with students and seniors

Glenna Orr

together. Once I felt settled with the classroom and my colleagues, I approached the school's principal, Dr. Carolyn Buckenmaier, about introducing an intergenerational program at White Oaks.

The experience gleaned from the three-year intergenerational partnership with the German retirement home suggested immense value for youth engaged in a volunteer activity. Instilling the interest to regularly volunteer, starting while children were quite young, can forever change the way people live their lives.

When I met with Dr. Buckenmaier to share my experiences working with students and German seniors, I sensed that I was talking with a kindred spirit. Dr. Buckenmaier was a truly gifted administrator who knew the importance of the long-term benefits to students from short-term extracurricular efforts, and she eagerly approved my plan to establish an intergenerational partnership between my class and a nearby retirement center.

It wasn't difficult to find a place to establish our new program. Right around the corner from White Oaks Elementary School was Burke Lake Gardens, an independent and assisted living retirement center. The residents of Burke Lake Gardens were a diverse group, representing several cultures, languages and nationalities. I was confident that my time overseas had proven that the innocence of a child's friendship could surmount any boundary. So, armed with my notes from Germany and the approval of my principal, I contacted the director of the facility. Finding the program site was easy; convincing the director to participate was not. Not surprisingly, she was very protective of her seniors, so the process of introducing my idea began slowly.

The facility director liked concrete, supervised programs and asked me what my intentions were for the program I was proposing. I explained that its aim was to build partnerships between her seniors and my students. Realizing that her buy-in was critical to the success of this endeavor, however, I told her that we could work together on structuring an appropriate program. With her approval, I started bringing my third graders to the facility.

What started off tentatively evolved into four years of wonder at Burke Lake Gardens. It was interesting—and heartening—to see the pattern of the German program repeated in Virginia. Clearly, the bonds that can be formed between seniors and young people are universal, and it's always the simplest activities that have the most far-reaching impact in solidifying those connections. After our initial "get to know you" visits, my students jumped right in. The third-grade students from White Oaks filled many, many afternoon visits to Burke Lake Gardens with crafting sessions, and lively conversations always filled the air.

As our visits continued, I noticed that the students, even as young as they were, began to treat their time with the seniors as much more than simply a school project. During the holidays, the youngsters took it upon themselves to create a talent program for the residents and encouraged their parents to bake holiday goodies to make the occasion even sweeter. In fact, one of my fondest memories from my time at Burke Lake Gardens was the sight of my third-graders gathered around a piano singing "Have Yourself a Merry Little Christmas." As they listened to the song, the seniors' faces conveyed their own recollections of happy and sad times past. Through smiles and tears, the children made those feelings possible.

As each year passed, our relationships seemed to become more and more of an extended family affair. In addition to their school day visits, many of the children began to visit the center on their own after school—including weekends and during the summer months when it was not in session—often bringing along their parents, brothers and sisters. It was wonderful to watch the youngsters become true volunteers and develop a strong sense of ownership in building relationships with their senior companions. This was a community partnership that changed, endured, delighted, developed and strengthened as each year passed.

I'm very fortunate that some of my former students—now adults themselves—still keep in touch and update me on where life is taking them. The years have flown by quickly and much has happened in their lives, yet these young men and women were so moved by their experiences at Burke Lake Gardens years ago that they still like to share their fond memories of the valuable time they spent there as volunteers. This is where we meet Melissa:

Most children spend their elementary lives getting up, going to school, coming home, watching TV, doing homework, eating dinner and then going to bed to repeat the same routine the next day. I, however, in addition to many others who had Mrs. Orr as their third grade teacher, were fortunate enough to break that mold, having a great opportunity to experience first-hand the other things that our community had to offer.

As a third-grader, I spent time doing the typical third-grader things. But in addition, I went and visited with the elderly residents at Burke Lake Gardens to play games, put on plays, sing songs and even just to sit and talk with them. That's a pretty big thing for a third-grader. But looking back, it was so beneficial for both myself and them. Being able to spend time, tell them about school and what I was learning and hearing stories from their childhoods and growing up was one of the neatest things, especially since my extended family lives far away. It was kind of like having another grandmother and grandfather in a way, which was something that was very special to me.

One of the things that I will never forget is the Memorial Day play that we put on for both our school and for the retirement home. I remember being on stage and looking out at the seniors with smiling faces, realizing that many of them had spent some of their lifetimes serving our country. It was such an honor, and I was so proud that along with my classmates we were able to not only bring back a little nostalgia, but also to show some appreciation for everything that they had done for us and for our country—even though it was long before our time.

My year in third grade is most definitely the year that stands out in my childhood memories. In fact, I don't think I missed a day of school. Mrs. Orr was hands down the best teacher and one of the best mentors that I have met in my 23 years. She put so much of herself into everything she did for our class, and I know each and every one of us is so much better for it. I will never forget everything she has taught me both in and out of the classroom.

During the four years that I continued this program with my subsequent classes of third graders, we lost a few of our senior friends to death. It was an intriguing, sensitive experience for both students and parents, who had also developed relationships with the residents. In spite of the ups and downs, my students tended to not want to end the experience at the conclusion of each school year. Many times, I would take my students who had moved on to fourth grade back to Burke Lake Gardens with their parents for follow up visits. It was so wonderful to see friendships that were made with the seniors during the previous school year carryover with the students as they moved forward in their educations.

Chapter Three

On the Road Again

Brisas del Mar, Panama

If I've learned anything in life, it's to expect the unexpected. Just when life is headed in one direction, things happen that can grab a person by the shoulders and spin him or her around in a completely new direction. That's exactly what happened to my family in 1993, the year my husband was transferred to Panama from his military post at the Department of State.

Open Minds, Open Hearts

My children, now in high school and college, were becoming pros at making themselves at home in new places, so it was—thankfully—with little difficulty that they adapted to their new home. Once again, I was fortunate to find a teaching position, at the Department of Defense School at Howard Air Force Base, Panama, and resumed my career with a rambunctious class of kindergarteners. I still believed that their classroom learning could only be enhanced by introducing volunteer experiences to their curriculum, so I began to search for opportunities to pair their friendliness and eager energy with people in need.

It was soon thereafter that a Panamanian friend introduced me to Brisas del Mar. This place, on a tiny penninsula near Panama City, is home to the neediest of the needy Panamanian seniors. In fact, the residence that now served as a retirement home came into existence as a leper colony founded by the British in the 1800's. I sensed immediately that this was a unique place that could yield a special experience for my students. My presumption was verified when I met the facility's director, Sister Gerri Brake.

Sister Gerri is a Maryknoll nun who was stationed in Panama and administered the facility through the support of the Ministries of Panama. We connected almost instantly, and it was with great enthusiasm that she welcomed my students into her residents' home.

Glenna Orr

We entered this experience with some concern, as ten of the residents at Brisas del Mar were afflicted with leprosy. Our hesitation dissolved when we learned that the disease is not contagious, but I was still concerned that the sight of the patients might be more than my kindergarteners could absorb. I could not have been more wrong. The students displayed great bravery in working with these seniors in distress, and the heartening scene of these 5- and 6-year-olds hugging these needy residents was a sight to behold. And the friendships they formed were truly special.

One of the residents, Gwendolyn, was blind, yet had a great love of music, evidenced by a talent for playing the tambourine. Rather than simply play songs for the children, Gwendolyn shared her talent with the youngsters by teaching them to play the instrument. They crafted their new skill to the point they could lead songs on the tambourine and would put on special musical performances for the residents. Another senior, Amielda, age 86, was one of the older residents and had a fondness for cats. Her feline family included 12 cats of various breeds and ages, and she loved them dearly. The kindergarteners enjoyed visiting Amielda and playing with her cats while listening to her light-hearted stories and jokes. This intergenerational experience represented the epitome of graciousness between youth and seniors who represented not only two different demographics, but also, as in the case of my German experience, two different traditions: "American" and "Hispanic." It was so encouraging to see yet again that barriers that might seem obvious and complicated were not an issue. The children worked with the seniors manicuring gardens together, singing songs and providing hours of selfless friendship. They were right at home in this unique place.

Part of what made it so special was the care and dedicated administration from Sister Gerri. I was a guest in this country, yet felt so much a part of her courageous efforts. She, too, has expressed fond memories of how the kindness of my students brought happiness into the lives of her residents:

From the fall of 1993 to the spring of 1994, Glenna and her young companions enhanced the quality of our lives. It is difficult to decide who enjoyed the weekly visits more: the impressionable children or the grateful elderly men and women. LOVE was in practice through the children's generous gesture to visit us in an ongoing fashion. Simplicity and innocence were shared.

Our oceanfront setting with an open park provided the afternoon atmosphere of visiting and touching through hugs and handshakes. The children attended the green area by weeding the

Glenna Orr

garden and raking our leaves. Watching children motivated by love touches the heart. The group had a great idea to visit the rooms of each resident. One child observed that the residents lacked plant life in their rooms. Shortly after, all residents were given a plant for their rooms. Dear Edelmira, a tiny, fragile 89-year-old woman was delighted. She understood the instructions for the afternoon sun to mean for her to daily take her plant outdoors for two hours. She faithfully sat beside the plant, watching it grow. She fascinated the children, and although she could barely communicate due to a stroke, she communicated volumes to the children by her preciousness. She loved her plant.

Then there was Gwendolyn, an 87-year-old blind and bilingual African-American woman. She had no family to visit her, so the children became her family. They sat with her on her bed. Her laughter and interest in them were gifts to be received. The children learned about her love of music, and she played the tambourine at the daily liturgies. For Christmas, the children surprised Gwendolyn with a gift of a new tambourine for her personal use. This instrument became her pride and joy.

Both Edelmira and Gwendolyn died in 1997 well accompanied and loved. They left us with happy memories. To know them was to love them. This is the mutual experience that volunteers receive when they give of themselves. The intergenerational bonds serve [to teach] each generation not to fear the natural aging process, but to realize that love is for all ages.

If time and circumstances would have allowed, I could have lived a contented life in Panama working side by side with Sister Gerri. But she was not the only special person I met on this journey. Jean Lamb, principal of a Department of Defense School in Panama, was supportive of our program at Brisas del Mar and encouraged every opportunity for her students to extend themselves beyond the traditional education sphere. Her recollections are particularly special to me:

Each school year students, parents and teachers join together to design activities that enrich the students' lives. Of course, schools tend to emphasize the academics and integrate community social activities. When caring, thoughtful teachers and parents put their heads

Glenna Orr

together, they plan activities for their students that integrate social learning activities that support community institutions. That is just what happened when kindergarten teacher Glenna Orr and fifth grade teacher Don Kinghorn developed a program for their students to visit and interact with elders in Brisas del Mar, an elder care facility in Panama City, Panama.

Frequently, the students went to the retirement home to sing, share stories and do projects together. The students learned from the retired adults about their earlier lives in Panama and shared skills that they had to offer the children. The children learned that their elders had much to offer them by sharing and participating in activities that were enjoyed by all of them. Age does not make much of a difference when you have an opportunity to come together for the joy of interacting with other people. The sharing time was a marvelous experience for everyone involved.

Chapter Four

Florida State University (FSU)

1994-1995

Our time in Panama was brief yet fulfilling. Once again, saying goodbye to my students and senior friends was difficult. Yet I was thankful for having had the opportunity to use what I had learned to teach the students in my class how they could bring happiness and enjoyment to people in need.

Upon our return to the states, my family settled in Tallahassee, Florida. Again entering the job market in a new area, I was directed to the Florida State University Developmental School. "Developmental school" is a fancy way of describing a research school. The student body was made up of a very diverse group of youngsters. They were largely children of the university's scholars as well as children from the local community. The students' eclectic backgrounds made for rich learning environment and allowed their eyes to be opened to different ways of life.

The school administrators knew of my background in intergenerational programming, so during the interview process, I was asked about the possibility of starting such a program at their school. I responded that I could; based on my previous experience, I assumed it wouldn't be too difficult. I also stipulated that, if chosen for a teaching position, my son Ryan would be admitted to the school. There was a lengthy waiting list for the FSU Developmental School. But given that we were just getting established in a new town, I felt it important that Ryan have some kind of comfort zone in yet another new school.

There were hundreds of applicants for only two teaching positions, and I was fortunate to have been chosen to teach fifth grade. While I was excited to get the job, this would prove to be a challenging assignment, as this particular group of students had a reputation for being difficult to handle. I would soon learn that my duties would extend far beyond the classroom.

Tallahassee is not a large town, so I assumed it would not be difficult to locate senior residence facilities to begin my inquiries about starting another intergenerational program. How fortunate I was, though, to find The Arbors of Tallahassee, a new facility with a young, energetic director who jumped at the opportunity to partner with my class and supplement the programs she offered her residents.

Establishing the connection with the facility administrator proved to be the easy part of the process this time around. What took some time and extra effort was securing the trust of my new students and ensuring them that this would be a positive, enriching experience. An important difference with this program was that it was the first time I partnered students with a facility specifically for seniors who were medically very needy. Most of them required some form of complete care, for strokes and other illnesses.

The seniors themselves took a little convincing, too. When we first began our bi-monthly visits, only two or three residents visited with the students. Over time, however, the word spread and the number of participants began to climb. Due to the nature of the care given at the facility, it was not always possible for residents to venture out of their

Glenna Orr

rooms to mingle with the students. So the youngsters often visited room to room to check on the more infirm patients, even if it was just to say hello. Although difficult, my fifth graders were mature enough to see past the duress of the patients and form friendships that resulted in the two generations working on crafts, telling stories and singing songs together. Young people can learn so much compassion from these trying experiences and learn to embrace the need to willingly offer help to others.

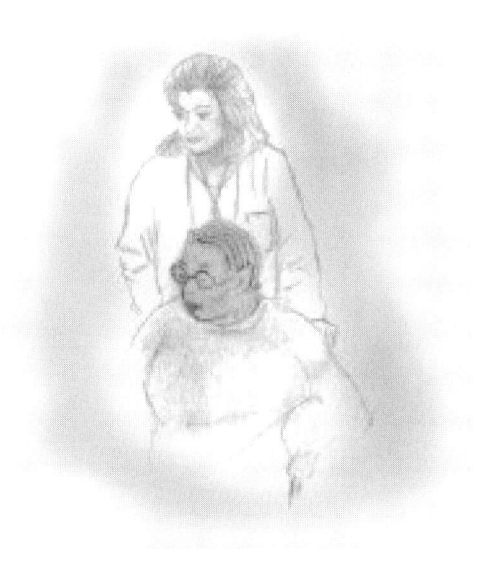

My favorite example of the sense of selfless giving that my students developed over this year-long program was the Valentine's Day party they hosted for Arbors residents in February 1995. The youngsters planned special Valentine's Day crafts to work on with their senior friends. Everyone assembled in the facility's dining room to unveil tables specially decorated with red, white and pink tablecloths and linens. The walls were lined with special decorations. No party would be complete without treats, so the students (with the help of their parents) baked cupcakes and other goodies to share with the residents. To add to the fun, we recruited a local musician to perform for the group, much to the delight of the residents. The students didn't want anyone to feel left out of the fun, so those residents who were confined to their wheelchairs enjoyed several twirls around the room to the beat of the music. Fifth-graders tend to be a bit goofy, but their wheelchair dancing was anything but. It was just another way that the students showed how much they valued their relationships with the residents of the Arbors.

Admittedly, moving to Tallahassee from Panama was not my first choice. I had hoped to go to Charlotte, North Carolina, and had even received a job offer and enrolled my son in school there. However, my husband needed to be in Tallahassee, so that's where our family settled for the time being. I was not disappointed, though, at the end of the school year when it appeared that my family was headed back to the Washington, D.C., area. This was a difficult year at times. But looking back on it now, I realized that we were there for a reason. My volunteerism helped to bring some sense to my life at

Glenna Orr

the time and most definitely the lives of a very energetic and diverse group of students. Even though it was only a year, I hope it was a year that made at least some small difference in the lives of my students and their senior companions.

Chapter Five

Washington Mill and The Fairfax at Belvoir Woods

Fairfax County Public Schools
1995-1998

The old saying is true: there's no place like home. Though my family's experiences abroad and short stints at new places in the states were enjoyable and served a purpose in our lives, I was thrilled at the prospect of returning to Fairfax County Public Schools in the fall of 1995. I had an opportunity to

Glenna Orr

resume third grade teaching duties, but this time at a new school, Washington Mill Elementary. Teaching third grade students was a welcome commitment for me, but with my family once again re-establishing itself in Northern Virginia, I intended to not spread myself too thin. To me, this restriction included not starting an intergenerational program at Washington Mill. My family required my time and attention that year, so I didn't think it selfish that I "just" wanted to be a teacher, a role that requires full-time attention as it is.

So much for planning. Shortly after I started at Washington Mill, the school community got wind of my previous experiences, and it asked that I make an intergenerational program happen. I resisted at first, but must admit that I missed spending time volunteering with my students. Returning to the Northern Virginia area and teaching at a new school, I wasn't sure which facilities were close to the school or which would even be interested in hearing from me. So I contacted my dear friend Shirley Segal, director of Burke Lake Gardens, who had been such a wonderful partner when I administered the intergenerational program at White Oaks Elementary School. Shirley enticed me to become acquainted with The Fairfax at Belvoir Woods, a retirement center that was home to several retired military officers and senior Foreign Service officers. It was previously owned and operated by The Marriott

Open Minds, Open Hearts

Corporation and subsequently owned by Sunrise Senior Living. It sounded like a perfect fit for my students. So I set out, once again, to make a match between students and seniors.

A match was made and a new and endearing program began. Part of what made this experience so memorable was the enthusiasm and joy with which my students' parents embraced the program. They became true partners in it and I'm forever thankful for their support. It's difficult to summarize three years of wonderful memories, but I've tried, nonetheless. Here are just a few of those special memories from our partnership with the wonderful residents of The Fairfax.

As our first school year of visits drew to a close, my students wanted to make Memorial Day a special celebration for their new senior friends. It's easy to think that the significance of this holiday is lost on the young, but my students' actions demonstrated that this was not the case. Their plans for a special Memorial Day program were sincere and heartfelt and their parents outdid themselves in support of this gathering. The parents surprised us with cookies, brownies and other goodies, as well as traditional red, white and blue memorabilia. American flags were visible everywhere and the spirit of patriotism was palpable. My students, along with several parents representing each branch of the military service, sang beautiful songs saluting our

Glenna Orr

men and women in the Armed Forces. The seniors' faces showed their appreciation, which gave way to tears when two of third grade boys offered impromptu salutes at the end of the presentation. I, too, was moved by the boys' earnest expressions as they saluted the seniors. I'm not quite sure they understood the significance of their gesture, but I'm sure they knew it was the best way they could convey their respect for and comprehension of the importance of Memorial Day.

As my second school year at Washington Mill began, I met a new group of eager third graders. My "alumni," however, were still very much in the picture, as they wanted to continue their visits to The Fairfax. Building on their volunteer experiences from the year before, this group of seasoned fourth grade volunteers had the confidence and experience to mentor my new third graders and introduce them to the residents of The Fairfax.

The year proved to be a special experience for parents and students alike and I was pleased that the Washington Mill community continued to embrace the program. One student who comes to mind when I think of this time is Brett, and I can't think of Brett without thinking of his mother, Lauren. She was an active volunteer alongside Brett. Her recollections offer a glimpse of the dynamic between students, parents and seniors that year.

When my son, Brett, was in the third grade, his teacher, Mrs. Glenna Orr, had his class volunteer at The Fairfax retirement home in Ft. Belvoir, Virginia. Every Wednesday after school, I would drive a group of students to The Fairfax. There they would work on crafts with the seniors. Over time, Brett developed a special friendship with Colonel Ray Higgins, one of the retirees. They would talk and work on crafts together, and after time, became quite close.

Glenna Orr

At the end of the year, the retirement home awarded a "Circle of Love" award to Brett for his "exceptional compassion, patience and kindness" that he showed Colonel Higgins. Colonel Higgins came to the school and presented the award during the end of the year ceremony. I was very proud of my son, and very happy to be able to be a part of a program that helped our children learn the importance of volunteering with seniors.

As a teacher, I can encourage my students to tap their abilities, strive for their goals and share their talents with others. But, the prime motivating force in their lives remains their parents. That's why I was so fortunate that the parents of my students took ownership of the volunteer program at The Fairfax. In fact, the parents themselves became volunteers along with their children and, in the process, became equally attached to our friends at The Fairfax. As with their children, the volunteerism made a difference in their lives. The recollections of Joan Knetemann, another parent, offer a perfect example:

> *Glenna Orr taught my son, Michael, in third grade. An integral part of her class was participation in the intergenerational program at The Fairfax. Michael and I were regular attendees at the twice-monthly outings. It was an experience that has made my life richer. I wish all our children had the opportunity to work with senior citizens the way Michael and I were able to do.*
>
> *One of my favorite residents was "Mary." She was a little Irish-American woman with a twinkle in her eye. While Michael visited with his "Colonel," I would sit and listen to Mary reminisce about her life. She was an artist and had a beautiful collection of paintings and collectibles from around the world. Chatting with Mary was a wonderful respite from my busy driving days. At The Fairfax, time seemed to stand still and, for a short time, you could do what was right, not*

Glenna Orr

what was necessary. Visiting the residents of The Fairfax taught all of us, parents and children, to take time to talk and listen to each other.

While I was thrilled that the parents not only took an interest in the program and also established relationships of their own, it's the stories of the students that I find truly inspiring. One story that warms my heart even now is that of Lindsey and Mrs. Kluge. It's best told in Lindsey's own words:

My parents have always taught me that you don't truly know what something is like until you have tried it for yourself. Many times I have found this lesson to be true. When I was in third grade, in Mrs. Orr's class at Washington Mill Elementary School, my mom told me once again, "Try it, you might like it." Mrs. Orr's classes went once every two weeks to an assisted living home, The Fairfax at Belvoir Woods. My mom was a room parent and wished to volunteer, so I sort of got dragged along. When I was in the third grade, like most kids that age, I didn't rebel much. I maybe cried twice, tried to change their minds, got the point that I had lost and moved on with my life.

During the first visit to The Fairfax, I met a woman named Evelyn Kluge. Mrs. Kluge had decided spur of the moment to join the other residents in doing arts and crafts with the students from my class, much as I had. At first I was very reserved, and so was she, but we both opened up. I am not exactly known as a "people person," and I wouldn't consider social work as my life goal or anything, but I really enjoy helping people. Mrs. Kluge was no exception. But, like so *many other things that are enjoyable and entertaining, it didn't feel like helping. It felt almost like laughing with an old friend, just with both senses of the word "old." As we went back several other times, I always found Mrs. Kluge. We made several neat things together, and I still have some of the Christmas decorations we made together.*

When we went to make the crafts, we had to know ahead of time exactly what to do. The children were essentially the ones in charge when making the crafts, which was fun for all of us. Now that I think about it, I don't think the residents of The Fairfax really cared; they just enjoyed being around us and laughing with us. And after all my reservations about going the first time, I never missed going to The Fairfax. Mrs. Kluge came every time, too. There is something universal about naïve and innocent children and older, dependent senior citizens. Without realizing it, I had helped Mrs. Kluge have something to look forward to and to remember fondly afterwards. And, as I was quick to admit, I looked forward to it also.

Then, in the spring of 1998, Mrs. Kluge's health took a turn for the worse. When we went to The Fairfax that week, Mrs. Kluge was not at our usual table in the dining room where we made crafts. I asked where she was, and I was taken to her room. She was in bed; she had become very weak and couldn't get up out of bed. She had actually asked to see me when I came, but they left it up to me. I went to see her, held her hand and talked to her. I remember seeing how black and blue her hands were and how bruised she was all over. I didn't know what it meant then.

Two days later, Mrs. Kluge passed away. My family sent flowers to her children. About two weeks later, we received a letter from her children telling us how much I had meant to her and how much she had looked forward to seeing me. Back then, I didn't really pay that much attention to it. I'm sure I was like, "Oh...that's nice. So can I go outside and play?" But now that really means something. If everyone unselfishly helps just one other person in their lifetime, imagine how much nicer the world would be.

Glenna Orr

The Washington Post came to write a story on Mrs. Orr's class about a week after Mrs. Kluge died. When they were talking about The Fairfax, I just started sobbing. This was the first time as a child I had ever experienced the death of a relative or someone close to the family, and Mrs. Kluge was as good as my adoptive grandmother. I remember they had a little blurb [in the Post] about how sad I was and how I had cried. We had not gone to Mrs. Kluge's funeral, and I had no chance to really come to terms with the fact that she was not going to be there the next time I went to The Fairfax. When they were asking about Mrs. Kluge, it hit me. It really hit me. Most children don't really understand what death is, but they have some concept of "forever" and "never." And I knew I would never see Mrs. Kluge again and that she was gone forever.

Going to The Fairfax with Mrs. Orr's third grade class was a wonderful and bittersweet experience for me. I really enjoyed helping others, and it taught me the meaning of being selfless. My mom and I still have those "remember when" moments, and often we talk about The Fairfax and Mrs. Kluge. One time recently, my mom remembered that I hadn't wanted to go. "Aren't you glad you ended up going?"

Yes, I am.

Chapter Six

Making a Promise

Macfarland Middle School
1998-1999

This was a particularly difficult year for me and, once again, I relied on volunteering to provide me with a needed sense of comfort and some perspective in my life. This is the year that I lost my beloved father to a severe illness. He was not just a parent; he was my dearest friend in the world and someone who personafied unconditional love. It's because of his support that I had the confidence to extend myself into new areas and try to do what I could to help others. Losing this truly special man was devastating. However, in spite of the sadness my family experienced at this time, I could see yet again how life is a balancing act. When one door closes, another one opens.

I didn't realize it at the time, but the door that opened came via an invitation from a national nonprofit organization based in Alexandria, Virginia. It was seeking to develop a model for intergenerational programs. America's Promise—The Alliance for Youth is a broad-based group whose members work together to ensure that all young people can realize their full potential. The Alliance works to accomplish this goal by ensuring all young people have the five essential resources—known as the Five Promises—that they need to thrive in life: caring adults who are actively involved in their upbringing; safe places in which to learn and grow; a healthy start toward adulthood; an effective education that builds marketable skills, and opportunities to help others. Founded by retired General Colin L. Powell following the Presidents' Summit for America's Future in 1997, the America's Promise Alliance includes nonprofit, corporate and community groups as well as individuals nationwide. The more I learned about America's Promise, the more enthused I became about its mission and the Five Promises, particularly opportunities to serve. Volunteerism is an important component of a holistic education. I had been trying to foster that in my students long before I became acquainted with America's Promise.

It was an honor to be asked to share my experience in this field with a newly-formed national organization seeking to establish its roots and create program models that could be replicated across the country. Before the program could go national, though, we'd have to test it at the local level. The staff at America's Promise identified a school in need of assistance—Macfarland Middle School in Washington, D.C. This school, serving students in grades six through eight, has a large minority population; nearly all of the students qualify for free or reduced lunches. The students' needs were great, but I've never been one to resist a challenge. With the school identified, it was up to me to find a retirement center to partner with these special students.

Through my network of connections and some independent research, I learned of the Soldiers' and Airmen's Home in Washington, D.C. It's always difficult to predict with complete accuracy whether a residence and a school will be a good fit, so I followed my instincts (and crossed my fingers). My prayers could not have been more fully answered. There was a strong synergy that produced a mutually enriching experience for students and seniors alike. Thankfully, the young people and their teacher were highly motivated and genuinely sincere with this intergenerational effort. Equally gracious, the residents of the Soldiers' and Airmen's Home opened their doors and hearts to us, and we danced right in.

As with the programs in years past, this particular placement offered a slight twist on what I had done before. And once again, the maturity and compassion of the students astounded the adults shepherding them through the program. The Soldiers' and Airmen's Home (now known as the Armed Forces Retirement Home) had a special wing dedicated to caring for 14 patients in progressing stages of Alzheimer's disease. This was a very contained area of the facility to ensure the safety of the patients, with only one way in and one way out of the wing. Due to the severity of their conditions, these residents were not able to join our group when it met for its bi-monthly visits. The students knew about this community of residents but had not been given the opportunity to interact with it. To be completely honest, I wasn't sure the middle schoolers would be equipped to handle the (at times) unpredictable moods and behavior of Alzheimer's patients. I didn't discourage the students' curiosity; I simply tried to help them focus on developing relationships with the seniors who participated in our regular visits.

As our visits continued and the youngsters' confidence grew, they became more and more interested in meeting the Alzheimer's patients. It

Glenna Orr

was with reluctance that I finally agreed. I approached the administrator with the students' request. Soon thereafter, we made our way to a remote wing of the facility to meet these special patients. I was pleased to see the visit unfold as so many others before it had. These spirited middle schoolers, their passionate teacher and I crafted, talked, visited and shared many, many smiles with the Alzheimer's residents. These seniors seemed to respond positively to their young visitors, and we loved every minute of our time with these dear people.

Open Minds, Open Hearts

As the school year drew to a close, my students, who had demonstrated themselves as able volunteers throughout the course of their visits, were asked to assist with a special project. The director of activities at the Soldiers' and Airmen's Home had worked closely with the students and me. She announced during one of our volunteer activities with the Alzheimer's patients that a Hawaiian luau was going to be held on the campus of the Home and that she would like to include her very severe Alzheimer's patients. The activities director needed our help to make that possible. Once again, my students stepped up to the plate and did what needed to be done.

On the day of the luau, we all headed to the Alzheimer's wing and guided the patients to a bus to take them to the event. I vividly remember some anticipation on our part; those of us who were assisting hoped that things would go smoothly—and they did. With a full bus, we drove across campus and entered a room decorated with flowers and Hawaiian island motif. The setting was so pretty, and to add to the theme, we were all given colorful leis to wear as we entered the room.

For the "field trip," we were guided and instructed on what to expect and what would take place with the patients, especially because this was the first time we were taking them out of their usual environment. The Macfarland students were magnificent! To watch the students "play" with the Alzheimer's patients was divine! We danced, laughed, enjoyed fruit punch and ate delicious food. The gathering was not without challenges; Alzheimer's patients who are mobile will wander. But the guidance and supervision that we provided helped to keep the evening on course. One of the most honorable efforts I recall from that evening was how we were able to help provide a necessary level of comfort for the Alzheimer's patients, who had left behind their familiar world.

This was a special event on so many levels. The seniors enjoyed a much-anticipated trip out of the facility; the two generations had an opportunity to socialize beyond the bounds of a typical after school visit, and the Alzheimer's residents were brought into the wider Home community. As we ate, danced and laughed that evening, I couldn't help but be inspired by the Macfarland students. They were sensitive, intuitive and wise beyond their years. Without fail, they dedicated their time and effort to this precious group of seniors and made some lasting friendships in the process.

Open Minds, Open Hearts

The Macfarland experience came along during an emotionally trying point in my life. I've long believed, though, that keeping busy is my saving grace and that having a mission helps anyone give his or her best to everything around him or her—even when it seems like there's nothing left to give. Still, I look back on my time with these special seniors and young people as a double-edged sword. While it was inspiring to see the students blossom through their interactions with the residents, I couldn't help but draw parallels between the delicate Alzheimer's patients and my own father's rapidly declining health. I recall thinking on several occasions, "I hope he never gets to this point." Looking back, though, I'm so grateful to have had the

Glenna Orr

experience. Whether they realized it or not, this group of middle schoolers offered a treasured example of how to put life in perspective. They helped prepare me for the loss of my father, my wonderful best friend.

Chapter Seven

Carl Sandburg Middle School

1998 – 2000

My father's passing and beginning the program at the Soldiers' and Airmen's Home coincided with another major career event: transferring to a new school. Upon completion of my (second) master's degree in reading from Virginia Tech, I earned my certification as a reading specialist. The administrators of Fairfax County Public Schools requested that I transfer to Carl Sandburg Middle School in Alexandria to help develop the school's

Glenna Orr

reading department. I knew from the outset that this was going to be a challenge. Developing the reading program didn't mean refining one that already existed; it meant starting from scratch to create a program that could be adaptable to students of varying reading abilities, including those with challenges ranging from learning disabilities to those for whom English was not their primary language. In short, I was being hired to help bridge the gap for students making the transition from elementary to middle school who still needed structured reading help.

While attending classes at Virginia Tech, one of my professors suggested I pursue this opportunity as a way to not only broaden my professional experience, but also to expand the reach of my volunteer programs. I accepted the challenge with spirit and energy because I've enjoyed a lifelong love of reading and have tried to help my students discover the joy of good books. But a significant part of what excited me most about this placement was the opportunity to introduce a new set of students to another kind of joy: volunteering. What evolved was a wonderful combination of my two passions.

When I transferred to Carl Sandburg, the intergenerational program at Washington Mill ended. So I was eager to begin again at my new school. Because the nature of our work was primarily remedial, teaching these students required a combination of patience, tender loving care and strong instruction. Though I was not their primary instructor, my interaction with the students was frequent and intense, which allowed us to form solid working relationships. I was hopeful that this dynamic would convey beyond the classroom to volunteerism, yet mindful of the challenges that lay before us.

Once again, the eagerness of young people impressed me. My reading students at Carl Sandburg became my new partners at The Fairfax at Belvoir Woods. They were a small yet remarkable group of volunteers. I was thankful for their willing participation and dedication as parental support was lacking, largely due to the age of the students and many parents who worked long hours. So twice a month, we piled into my car and we were off to The Fairfax to write another intergenerational story.

One of my most cherished memories of this program involved a very special lady: Mrs. Helen Spencer. Mrs. Spencer was an independent living resident at The Fairfax whose home was a cottage on the facility's campus. In her 80s, she was sharp, active and ever so intuitive. She was also a talented artist. Mrs. Spencer was a widow and never had any children of her own, so her neighbors at The Fairfax comprised her social circle.

Glenna Orr

Shortly after my students began visiting The Fairfax, Mrs. Spencer expanded her circle a little wider by graciously inviting us into her home for visits. The children were immediately struck by her fantastic sense of style, as evidenced by the vivid colors that decorated her home, which was opulent yet comfortable. These visits evolved into art lessons and usually included special treats and snacks. Mrs. Spencer always treated the young people as proper guests. They responded in kind with their best manners and behavior. It was amazing to watch the students listen and learn; Mrs. Spencer certainly had a captive audience.

As their relationship developed, it was heartwarming to watch Mrs. Spencer become more like the students' surrogate grandmother than simply a friend. I remember during the holidays that year that Mrs. Spencer made it a point of throwing a mini-holiday party for the students, for which she prepared snacks and other Christmas goodies. She even surprised the young people with a raffle-the prize was a piece of her original artwork. The anticipation was palpable as all of the students' placed their names in a hat and Mrs. Spencer drew the winner. As I reflect on this experience, though, it's easy to see that there wasn't only one winner-all of the students gained from getting to know Mrs. Spencer. So did I.

Chapter Eight

Northern Virginia Community College

2001-2003

Keeping busy has always been my saving grace. However, during the period that I was building the program at the Soldiers' and Airmen's Home and beginning a new job at Carl Sandburg Elementary School, I learned what "busy" truly meant. It was during that time that I also began teaching college freshmen as an adjunct professor in developmental reading, writing and English literature at Northern Virginia Community College.

Glenna Orr

Teaching new college students is something that I had always wanted to do, so when the opportunity presented itself, I couldn't say no, despite my other commitments.

College is a new beginning for students contemplating their futures—another threshold to cross in their educational careers and certainly a fresh opportunity to make a mark with their lives. While teaching this fragile age group, I couldn't help but offer them the opportunity to have some fun with our senior population—and that they did. For two years, my students at NOVA's Annandale Campus visited local retirement centers and volunteered their time and lovely souls to the equally lovely seniors. I would witness my students playing Bingo, participating in armchair aerobics, reading poetry, playing a game of indoor horseshoes, giving manicures and simply engaging in light-hearted conversation with their senior friends.

In addition to the students' eagerness to extend themselves to the local senior population, I was thankful for another special young woman. Isabel Castillejo, only in her 20s, was the director of the Annandale Adult Day Care Center, where we spent much of our time. Isabel was not much older than many of my students. Yet she possessed the wisdom of a seasoned professional who knew the mutually-enriching relationships that could be built between the college students and her seniors. It's wonderful to read her recollections of the experience.

My "folks" always loved when "the kids" came to visit. The partnership we had with Mrs. Orr's Northern Virginia Community College class was more than just putting together crafts. Five or six students would visit with five or six of my folks once a week for about an hour. Each time they would partner up one-on-one and work on a project together. Projects ranged from Halloween pumpkin painting to wood working.

Each of the seniors was paired up with students who we felt had similar personalities. My folks would always start off a bit standoffish, but with in minutes their faces would light up with energy given off by the students. When the students smiled, the seniors smiled. It was such a joy to see. Some days the projects didn't even get finished. After the first session, I realized that the project only became an icebreaker and second to a more important goal, socialization. Many of the folks hadn't spoken to a teenager since their children or grandchildren were teenagers.

Glenna Orr

One of my seniors only spoke Spanish, which closed her off to many conversations. I paired her up with a vivacious Spanish-speaking student and instantaneously she became this cheerful, talkative person who came right out of her shell. Finally, there was someone who understood her!

Throughout the students' time at the center, they opened up to our folks' wisdom.

Many of the conversations I overheard were of our seniors sharing advice about their schooling career, "When I was your age…." Eventually, the class ended and all the students moved on; however, one student continued to volunteer at our center once a week. She incorporated her job at a local bath and body store to a program she started and facilitated once a week at the center. She would bring in different hand creams and give several seniors a hand makeover. Every Thursday she could be seen walking in with her bag of lotions and an energetic smile on her face. She would sit at a table and work with one senior at a time. The two could be seen having conversations as if they were at a beauty salon. It was such a treat to our folks. She eventually moved away to school, but before she left she was able to attend our Volunteer Appreciation Day celebration and even brought her parents. The students touched the lives of our seniors and we were able to touch the lives of several students and maybe even inspire one into a career.

As we all know from our own educations, the lives of college freshmen are full of new experiences and are ever changing. Though these young adults likely would experience this volunteerism opportunity for only a brief time, the effort was worthwhile. Even if their participation was for just a semester, the students still had much they could share and much they could gain, including the passion to make volunteering a regular part of their adult lives. One particular student, Lina Jariri, stands out in my mind as an example of a life-long volunteer. I taught Lina for several semesters at NOVA; we still keep in touch as friends. I'm proud that she continued to volunteer her time to the seniors at Annandale Adult Day Care Center beyond her time at NOVA. I was even prouder when she was honored with a very special award for her dedication and commitment to the Center. But when you read Lina's thoughtful words about her experience, it's clear that earning awards was the last thing on her mind.

Glenna Orr

It was a great pleasure to volunteer at the adult day care center in Annandale, Virginia. Mrs. Orr was my English professor and she helped me get involved by giving a little back. I am currently a full—time student at American University. I stayed on board in the Adult Day Care for about a year, then I had to stop because of my class load. Mrs. Orr has inspired me as young adult to realize that these extraordinary individuals deserved to have attention, be able to interact with others and tell their life stories. I enjoyed all the moments shared...

I remember one of the ladies wanted to dance with my father—it was the funniest thing because my father for once turned bright red. I remember one special lady. I used to crush her food and feed it to her. Her name was Mrs. Nun. She was from Vietnam and didn't speak too much English, but body language says a thousand words. I remember all the times that Mrs. Nun would recognize me with welcoming arms. She was a cutie pie and I will always cherish deeply all the times that I spent with her. I believe *interacting with others of different backgrounds is a great learning experience to all ages, no matter who you are.*

Chapter Nine

> *I think volunteers are people who take time out of their plans just to help someone else. I'm really thankful for them!*

> *Volunteers donate their time and efforts to the student at Hollin Meadows.*

Hollin Hills

Fairfax County Public Schools
2003-2005

I thoroughly enjoyed teaching the next generation of educators during my time at Northern Virginia Community College, but there's nothing like teaching the eager, young minds of elementary school students. That's why I seized the opportunity to return to the elementary classroom as a reading teacher at Hollin Meadows Elementary School in Alexandria, Virginia. This is a very busy and highly rewarding position. It requires wearing many hats and assuming a number of responsibilities.

However, my job is made much easier by a special group of individuals.

When I arrived at Hollin Meadows Elementary School, I was thrilled to learn that the school had an active volunteer group called the Hollin Hills Volunteer Association, made up of seniors in the community. My principal, knowing that for many years I had established intergenerational programs at other schools, asked that I meet this volunteer group and work closely with it to develop ways for it to become more engaged in Hollin Meadows Elementary School. I considered myself fortunate to have been assigned this task; finding ways to use volunteers anxious to work is much easier than trying to recruit volunteers from scratch.

What a privilege it has been to meet such a wise, active and knowledgeable group of professional seniors. I currently have the pleasure of working with 16 volunteers who come to Hollin Meadows on a regular basis and greatly enhance the students' learning experiences through their generous contributions of knowledge and life wisdom. My favorite program (and my bias is showing here) is the literacy program that pairs seniors with students, some of whom need additional help reading and others who simply love to read. I think of it as an intergenerational book club. Each week, on Monday through Thursday, four ladies

Glenna Orr

meet with third-, fourth- and sixth-grade students in our school library during the students' recess periods and simply read together. Though it's a simple activity, the impact of the program has been significant. As part of the Virginia Young Readers Program, students and seniors read notable children's books and work together on related writing activities. Initially, the program began to help students who needed to spend more time on reading activities. Imagine my surprise when word spread among the students that this was a fun activity. Now students of all reading abilities want to be a part of this partnership. Considering that their participation requires the students to give up recess a few days each week, I take their interest as a high compliment!

> *I Think a volunteer is someone who helps you to be somebody you want to be.*

One of the things I've learned that's a constant across all of my intergenerational program experiences is that it takes dedicated volunteers not only to bring a program to life, but also to give it legs. Barbara (Bobbie) Seligman is one of those special people. As the coordinator of the Hollin Hills Volunteer Association, her dedication to education and the welfare of children is unsurpassed. Another benefit of working so closely with Bobbie is the strong friendship that we've developed. Just as the children do, I've learned that I have so much to gain from the experiences working with the seniors. Bobbie's extremely positive attitude and dedication to living each day to the fullest is admirable. Her optimism is contagious. I'll be forever thankful that she embraced the reading partnership at Hollin Meadows and put the full energy of the volunteer association behind it. It warms my heart to read her description of the experience.

This program has important goals, not the least of which is to encourage young readers, many of whom come from deprived environments, to enjoy reading for pleasure and to become acquainted with books of literary appeal. Further down the line, they may respond positively when they are told that they will read a Caldecott or Newberry award winner. As volunteers, it is rewarding for all of us to see how much pleasure is derived from our weekly reading aloud and discussion sessions. Nothing can substitute for this individualized encounter.

In time, our participants will become qualified readers and the satisfaction that comes from having read at least four of the nominated books at the elementary level is well worth the

Glenna Orr

effort. The collaborative effort of the faculty, staff members, students and community volunteers will broaden student awareness of literature as a life-long pleasure.

    Alongside Bobbie Seligman is Marjorie Ginsburg, who also dedicates so much time and effort to our literacy program. Marjorie's story is particularly special to me because of the relationship she has formed with her reading partner, Kenny. Kenny came to the reading group as a first grader, but needed much more than extra reading practice. Kenny's family had endured an unthinkable family tragedy that left adults in the family and greater community struggling for answers. This difficulty was magnified for Kenny, who joined our group as a shy, withdrawn, uncertain little boy. What he needed more than anything was the reassurance of a constant, friendly face. That's exactly what he found in Marjorie.

> *My volunteer is a good friend to me and a teacher, but mostly a friend.*

It was remarkable to watch their relationship evolve. Kenny and Marjorie were such a natural fit right from the start that there was never really any question about who he should be paired with—they seemed to pick each other. They must have known what they were doing, because when Kenny returned to the reading group in fourth grade, there was no doubt that he and Marjorie were going to be partners in reading again. That's the beauty of the students' relationships with their senior reading buddies: summer vacation can pass and when the two groups are reunited in the fall, they simply pick right up where they left off in June. They're like family relationships.

It's evident that this relationship matters to Marjorie, but it's also very important to Kenny. Often, young people his age take for granted the people in their lives. Not Kenny. Once when I asked my students to write their answer to the question, "What is a volunteer?" Kenny's response brought tears to my eyes. He described Marjorie when he wrote, "She's not just a volunteer. She's my friend, too."

In preparing for this project, I asked Kenny to write me a description of his experiences with Marjorie. I think his words say more than I ever could about the significance of their relationship.

Glenna Orr

[Mrs. Ginsburg] taught me how much fun reading is and how to read. Every time I don't know how to say a word, she tells me to go back and pronounce the word. Mrs. Ginsburg pushes me to different heights to read. Every time we read something funny, like when a character in a book does something funny, we laugh about it. Mrs. Ginsburg taught me since I was in first grade and now I'm in fourth grade. She taught me how to break words down and try to figure [them] out every time I read. Mrs. Ginsburg says I am getting better in reading. If you know my mentor Mrs. Ginsburg, you would know why she is a great reading teacher to me.

Mrs. Ginsburg is a good friend to me and a teacher, but mostly a friend. Every day I wish it was Tuesday and Thursday so we could read and have fun with books. I read with Mrs. Ginsburg every Tuesday and Thursday. I think that all kids should have a mentor like Mrs. Ginsburg. She is very nice and I hope when I leave elementary school other kids will get to read with her, too.

Kenny's mother Tammy also recognizes the unique friendship between Kenny and Marjorie:

I always thought that when Kenny learned how to read that's all he would do. He started out doing just fine and loved books, even if it was just to look at the pictures. Then he went through a terrible time in his life and everything changed. Kenny would not pick up a book or do much of anything else.

When he started reading with Ms. Ginsburg, he started reading slowly and would only read when he was at school. Now, three years later, he is asking me for books and magazines from the store and is reading at home. It's still slow going, but I think Ms. Ginsburg is a great influence on Kenny's life. He talks of her frequently with a smile on his face. He needed the extra help and a friend to read with.

Kenny and Marjorie's story is but one example of how the well-placed dedication of the senior volunteers is making a lasting difference in the lives of Hollin Meadows students. These young people become so much more than simply tutees to the

Glenna Orr

volunteers; they become an extension of their own families. Margaret Mayer, a six-year volunteer, sums up the sentiment quite simply:

I have eight grandchildren, and each year there are children with whom I read who are the same ages as one of my grandchildren. None of mine live [in the area], so by spending time in a similar school environment, I can share my grandchildren's school experiences.

It's also easy to hear a grandmother's pride in Barbara Shear, another of the Hollin Meadows volunteers. She described her experiences with her young friends:

I have always bragged about "my kids." First they were my own two daughters. Then, twelve years ago, "my kids" began to mean, at 4-year intervals, my three grandchildren. In the past few years, "my kids" has taken on an additional meaning—the small parade of third and fourth graders whom I have tutored at Hollin Meadows, our local elementary school.

Open Minds, Open Hearts

As members of a Foreign Service family in Africa, our girls usually went to international schools with racially and ethnically mixed, but economically privileged, student bodies. When we were on home assignments, Hollin Meadows School's population was made up mostly of privileged kids, along with smaller numbers of children from less affluent backgrounds, many of them of other races and ethnicities. Because of demographic changes and school redistricting, the proportions at our neighborhood school are now reversed.

The influx of immigrant families from many lands into the apartments and town houses along the nearby highway, and the inevitable aging of the population in our own middle class community, has resulted in a situation that can be beneficial to both groups. Daunting numbers of the school's students are from homes in which English is not the main language; others come from families so economically hard pressed that weary parents have little time or energy for homework supervision or volunteering. Their children often need some extra one-on-one help to succeed. That help takes time, and time is something their tightly scheduled teachers simply don't have. The active retirees of our neighborhood, on the other hand, have time and experience to spare. Those of us who have chosen to use that time and experience with the kids at Hollin Meadows have been richly rewarded.

One of the luxuries of being strictly a volunteer is that I don't have to worry about standard tests or work plans. When eyes glaze, and fidgets begin, I know the story doesn't speak to Ronda's frame of references or personal interests, and we scour the shelves of the reading room or library for something "cool" instead. If Ricardo likes tornados and natural disasters, we read and read about them until some phrase on a different subject intrigues him, and then our next book will be about...volcanoes. I learn that kids from other continents aren't automatically enchanted with stories about those places; bad memories sometimes prevail, and mutant ninjas hold more interest for Mansour than folk tales of his homeland. The repetition in the text of "The Gingerbread Man" gets a real belly laugh out of unsmiling Isaac, so I find more books with a repetitive chorus format to read over and over.

Whatever gets my kids interested and enthusiastic is what we read. Most of it is not great literature, but if it convinces them that reading is not only useful and necessary but sometimes can be almost as much fun as the latest video game (or in some cases, maybe even more so), then my retirement is on the right track.

To know that the volunteers and students consider their time together time well-spent refreshes me when my days in the classroom are long and arduous. It encourages me to continue working to make these magical matches between seniors and young people.

Closing Thoughts

> I think a volunteer could be a mom or dad, it can be an uncle to help you read or write. They can almost do any thing. A volunteer is a hero.

Merely a Pause and Not an End

Compiling 20 years of memories has been quite an experience. I've laughed, I've cried, I've reconnected and reminisced with old friends who've joined me at various stages of this journey. And I've heard from students—both current and former—in their own words describe how they've been touched by their experiences with intergenerational programs. I'm not so bold as to take credit for solely shaping their outlooks on the value of seniors and volunteerism in our society. Rather, I'm humbled if the time we've shared together made even the slightest difference in their lives. And it's their kind words—combined with those of the senior volunteers and other program participants—that drive me forward.

Many times throughout the process of compiling these memories, I've been asked by friends and colleagues why I wanted to tackle such a project. Those who know me know that I'm not wanting for things to do—I think every teacher can relate to that feeling. At first, I really didn't have an answer about why I wanted to write this book. It was something I just felt compelled to do. After 20 years of wonderfully inspiring, emotional and learning opportunities, why wouldn't I want to share the knowledge and insight I've gained with others? In my mind, to keep these experiences to myself would have been selfish.

My goals with this book, therefore, are simple and heartfelt: I want to inspire young people to enrich their lives through volunteerism and learning. I want to remind readers of all ages that seniors have so much to contribute to our society; they truly are our wisest teachers and we, as their students, have so much to learn from their experiences in the classroom of life. I also hope to show people of all ages what they can accomplish when opportunity and inspiration come their way. If this collection of stories can be used as a tool to convey those messages, then I'll consider this a mission accomplished.

That's not to say that I'm finished, though. Although these are the final pages of this book, I consider my teaching career, my volunteerism and the intergenerational programs I support very much works in progress. There will come a time when I'm personally satisfied that I've done all I can do and when that day comes, I'll be ready to begin a new chapter in my life. For now, however, I'm very much looking forward to what comes next in this chapter of my life.

*E*PILOGUE

A Daughter's Praise

Thoughts from Erinn

I was blessed to be the eldest child of such a special person with so many attributes.

Glenna Orr thought life was going to be the way she planned; however, this life threw her a curve ball. With the unknown, my mother rose to the occasion. She is never one to brag when it comes to her accomplishments, so I will share them with you. She not only made her own children her number one priority, she furthered her education in the evening to provide her children with many opportunities, while giving back to the community in various ways.

My mother, Glenna Orr, has been an educator since she finished her undergraduate work. Everywhere we resided-in the Republic of Panama; Frankfurt, Germany, Northern Virginia and Washington, D.C.,-she always made an indelibly positive impact on those whom she came in contact with, especially children.

Glenna Orr

My mother, wherever she is, will make eye contact with a six-, seven-, or eight-year-old child. There is this special communication I can't put into words. She will gain 100% of their attention, and she seems to be the only one in the room.

In addition to all of the teaching, mentoring of other teachers and being a reading specialist, she seemed to be drawn to many seniors who would thoroughly enjoy interaction with children.

So, one day without knowing how she really started and what she had up her sleeve, she began something not only special, but also something that she hopes to carry on forever.

Early in her career, she convinced the principal of her school to start an after-school program, uniting school-age children with seniors. They sang, did art projects, read with them and enjoyed each other's company. The program flourished. It began with just a few students, in several schools, catching the eye of The Washington Post and even people of higher stature.

I honestly believe these special educational programs have done well, not because this is something my mother learned in school, but because, it is simply a gracious gift she has been given.

Open Minds, Open Hearts

My mother has made such a difference and brought so much happiness to so many people it is almost magical. My mother believes there are several important things in life; family, health, the education of our youth. And, last but not least, reading.

Glenna Orr has educated, touched, changed lives and made a difference in our society.

When it comes to my mother, I know she has just begun…

~Erinn

$\mathcal{A}$PPENDIX

Starting an Intergenerational Program

Though each of my experiences starting intergenerational programs has had its own unique twist, the basic elements remain the same: people and time. The organizer needs time to devote to developing a program of substance and interest to both young people and seniors, as well as to developing a core group of volunteers to support the effort and promote its sustainability.

To start a program in a school setting, it's necessary to first secure the school administration's buy-in for the project. A program is much easier to run if the administration is behind it. Second, it's best to find a senior facility to visit that is in close to the school. Transportation can sometimes be an issue, so keeping close to the school makes it an easier drive for parents and other volunteers. Next, you've got to explain your program to the retirement facility staff and tell it what you're all about; it's much like presenting a resume at an job interview.

Once you start the program, it often proves itself. But if it doesn't, you must re-examine the situation and identify weak points. Perhaps the frequency of visits is an issue. It's important to be consistent. For example, you can't visit one month and then skip the next month. Seniors, especially those in nursing facilities, like to have a set schedule so they know when to expect visitors; a set schedule also assures consistent participation from children, parents and teachers.

If seniors and students are working together in one-on-one relationships, perhaps the matches aren't clicking. Some volunteers think that all students will immediately embrace the mentor/mentee dynamic, but that's not always the case. A match may work on paper, but you'll never know if it will truly take flight until the two participants meet and get to know each other. Sometimes the process of getting acquainted takes longer than others, and, just as in personal relationships, the match either works or it doesn't. If a pair doesn't seem to be a fit, don't hesitate to make the changes necessary to find a good match.

Inevitably, there will be the usual questions challenges. I've experienced plenty during my career. But it's the leaps of faith that we take in life that can make the most significant differences. If we don't take those leaps, life can be pretty boring and unfulfilling. So take a leap, extend your hand in

Glenna Orr

friendship and make the matches that make a difference. I'm willing to guarantee there are plenty of young people and seniors in your midst who would be grateful for the opportunity to get to know each other.

For additional information on Glenna's work and programs, visit her website: www.TheKindKids.org